SPECIAL, LITTLE YOU

Tristan Chancey

Special, Little You
Copyright © 2020 by Tristan Chancey

All rights reserved. No part of this publication may be reproduced, distributed, or transmitted in any form or by any means, including photocopying, recording, or other electronic or mechanical methods, without the prior written permission of the author, except in the case of brief quotations embodied in critical reviews and certain other non-commercial uses permitted by copyright law.

Tellwell Talent
www.tellwell.ca

ISBN
978-0-2288-4028-2 (Paperback)

The world is a big and beautiful place. The world needs every smile on every face.

The world needs all of your friends like me and special, little you. The world needs the not-so-nice friends too.

You mean something special to everyone.
Being you can be so much fun!

Your sweet laugh has the power to make spirits fly. When your friends feel low, you bring them up so high!

From each strand of hair on your little head, to every single word you've ever said, a mark is made on someone's heart. So, always be kind from the very start.

If you're ever sad or feeling blue, remember that people care for you: parents, friends, and teachers too!

When you remember who you are, the bright days are never far.

Doing your best could never be wrong.
Always remember that you are strong!
There are so many wonders to remember
about special, little you!

www.ingramcontent.com/pod-product-compliance
Lightning Source LLC
LaVergne TN
LVHW071655060526
838200LV00029B/464